Wildlife Rescue
Color and Learn
Costa Rica

For SIBU Wildlife Sanctuary

Karin Hoppe Holloway

My Fat Fox
MMXVI

My Fat Fox
86 Gladys Dimson House
London E7 9DF
United Kingdom

www.myfatfox.co.uk

Wildlife Rescue, Color and Learn, Costa Rica
© 2016 Karin Hoppe Holloway

Cover design © 2016 Karin Hoppe Holloway

ISBN 978-1-905747-48-1

To keep my promise.

This book is based on animals rescued
by the SIBU Wildlife Sanctuary.

Please color using any media
with your imagination!

Contents

HOWLER MONKEY

HOWLER MONKEY

Alouatta palliata palliate

Almost all of the monkeys in this book are Golden Mantled Howler Monkeys. In Costa Rica they are called Mono Congo.

They live in the lowlands with many interesting kinds of

insects and spiders,
birds and bats,
frogs and lizards and snakes,
skunks and raccoons and opossums,
sloths and tapirs,
anteaters and armadillos,
rodents and weasels,
and wild cats.

They also live with other fascinating kinds of monkeys such as the

Squirrel Monkey,
the Capuchin Monkey and
the Spider Monkey.

There 15 different species of Howler Monkey in the Americas. The Mono Congo is the largest. Males weigh about 22 pounds (10 kilos). They're about 2feet tall (0.6 m) and if you include their long tail – which is as long as their body and sometimes even 5 times as long– they're about 4 feet long (1.2 m). Females are a bit smaller than males but they're both about the size of a small dog with a very long tail. They live to be about 25 years old.

Each family, called a troop, is made up of about 18 monkeys. Normally, three of them are adult males. The rest, the females and their children, stay closely together on their own. They all hang about safe from predators in the treetops, peacefully snoozing and resting and relaxing nearly all day and night long.

Male Howler Monkeys loudly HOWL – louder than any other primate species in the world – at dawn to tell other troops of monkeys where they are and to keep away! They also howl throughout the day at other loud noises and before a heavy rain. When they howl together, they can be heard up to 12 miles away (20 km).

Mantled Howler Monkeys rarely walk on land – their home is high up in the canopy of the forest trees. They eat canopy leaves. They are able to grasp branches with their hands and feet as well as with their long tail – it's as long as they are. It's a prehensile tail – it can wrap around and hold onto branches, too. Their tail can also feel things just like their hands do. This is why they can rest, sleep and eat high up in the trees without falling down. They climb, walk and swing, run and leap, and stretch from branch to branch to make a bridge for other family members to travel over at the very top of the forest.

Howler Monkeys can even hang upside down to pick and eat leaves, flowers and fruit – and seeds. They eat 50 different kinds of leaves but their favorite meal is figs. They can smell ripe fruit and nuts from over a mile away (2 k) and see colors very well, which helps them find food. Howler poo is very important as it spreads seeds throughout the forest floor, growing new plant life there.

In the wet season, Howler Monkeys drink water left on leaves from the rain. They rub their hands in the water and then lick it off. In the dry season they have to go down to the ground to look for fresh water.

Mantled Howler Monkeys have no fur on their face. They have a flat nose with 'O' shaped nostrils. The males have black fur and the females have dark brown fur. Both of them have a reddish-brown golden fringe of longer 'guard' hairs that extend beyond the fur on the sides of their body. This looks like they're wearing a sleeveless coat, called a 'mantle'. This can even make them look like they're glowing. The babies are a silver color at birth. They turn golden after a few days and at 3 months they are the color of adults.

Howler Monkeys face many human threats to their survival. Humans cut down their forests to sell as wood. Then they burn what's left to create fields where they plant crops or build homes and condos. Humans build roads through their jungle, cutting down the monkeys' treetop 'roads'. Then the animals who use trees to travel on have to walk on land where dogs kill them. When they cross our roads, cars run over them. And the electrical lines that look like vines to travel on electrocute them. Even worse, humans take monkeys away to sell to zoos and some eat them as 'bushmeat'.

The ancient Mayan Civilization worshipped Howler Monkeys as beautiful gods. Now, more than half of the world's primates are endangered. Their rainforest homes are endangered, too. They need our protection to continue to survive.

The Howler Monkeys in this book are at SIBU to recover from accidents. SIBU lets them live in the sanctuary as they normally would in the wild, so that they can remain wild. When they return to the forest, they'll be healthy and normal.

CHARLIE
THE
ADULT HOWLER MONKEY

CHARLIE

Charlie is an adult male Howler Monkey. The males stay close to the females and children but they don't spend the day together. Charlie howls with the other males in his troop in the morning and then he checks out what's good to eat nearby in the treetops.

Charlie will hang either way, upside down or right-side up, to get the best leaves, flowers and fruit. His tail can feel things just like his hands and feet can feel them. Their tail is a 5th limb for Howlers – 2 arms, 2 legs and 1 tail.

The fact that Charlie doesn't need to come down from the treetops to poop and pee makes it very easy for him to enjoy himself where he's safe. People down below, though, need to remember this when walking in the forest!

MAX

THE

TEENAGE HOWLER MONKEY

MAX

Max is a teenager. When male juvenile Howler Monkeys are nearly adults, they are made to leave their troop and their home. Max is now healthy and ready to leave SIBU and return to the forest but first he'll need to join a new troop of Howler Monkeys. He is hanging out alone in the treetops, looking lonely and lazy, waiting for them to come along. He'll then join the troop and have a new family. This ensures a healthy population of Golden Mantle Howler Monkeys with a diverse gene pool. Without this, they cannot evolve.

MIC AND MAC
YOUNG HOWLER MONKEYS

MIC AND MAC

Little Mic and Mac are cousins. Their mothers and aunts and grandmas are nearby, also in the treetops, either resting and grooming each other or gathering a meal for all of them to enjoy. They all take care of each other. The young Howler Monkeys make a lot of noise as they run and jump and swing and play. Sometimes they also play with young Capuchin Monkeys.

MIA
THE
BABY HOWLER MONKEY

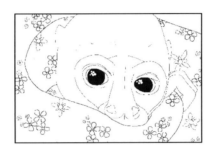

MIA

Baby Mia, all alone without her mother, has just been brought to the sanctuary at SIBU.

Very young baby Howlers cling to their mother's belly as she moves through the treetops, swinging on vines and walking on branches to look for food. When the baby grows bigger, it then rides on her back.

Where parts of the forest have been removed, there aren't any branches or vines to swing on. It's dangerous for her to walk on land so the mother has to use what's there to continue her journey to find food.

Many places in Costa Rica have electrical lines, above ground, that aren't sheathed – they're bare and dangerous. When she touches a bare electrical line that she thinks is a vine, the mother is burned so badly that the baby becomes a wounded orphan.

Baby Mia is wrapped warmly in a very soft blanket to make her feel comfortable again as she gets used to being without her mother. She'll be carried and cuddled, healed and cared for by the people working at SIBU until she is either adopted by another Howler female at SIBU or until she is well and old enough to join a new troop in the wild.

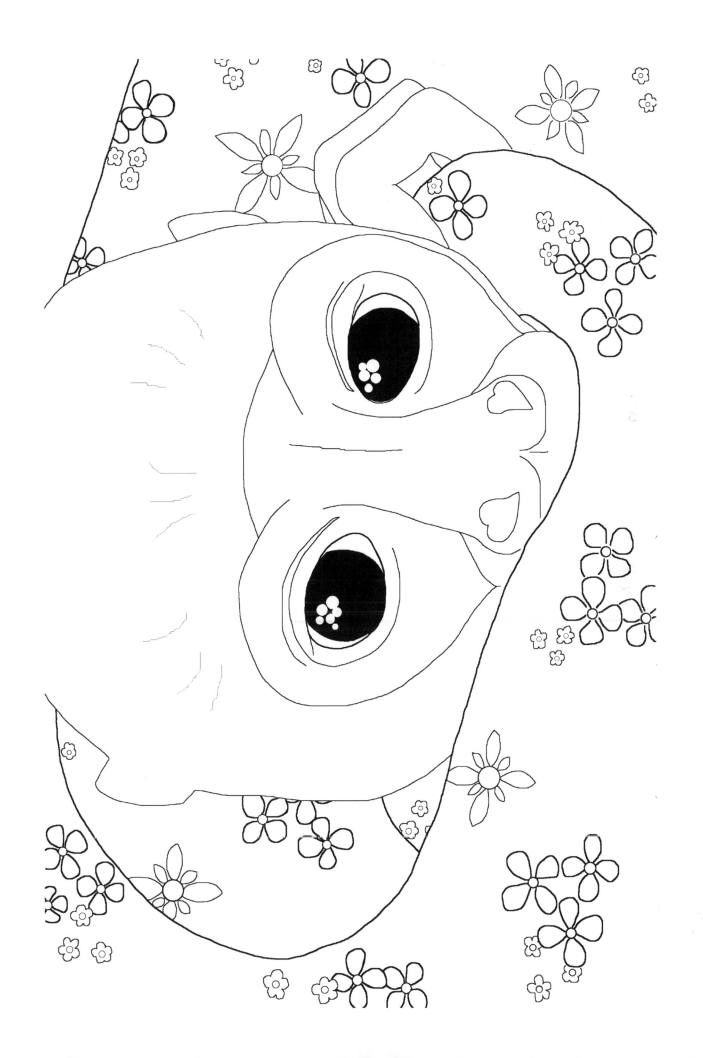

CAPUCHIN
MONKEY

CAPUCHIN MONKEY

Cebus capucinus

Capuchins first appeared in South America 16.3 million years ago. Humans and Capuchins are both primates and we share 97% of our DNA, our genetic code, with them.

Capuchin Monkeys are smart – they use tools. They use sticks to get to seeds and stones, as hammers and a hard surface to crack on, to break the hard shells of nuts to eat. They roll around in citrus oil, rubbing it into their fur, because insects don't like citrus oil. They make different warning sounds for each different threat to their group using sharp whistles, barks, coughs and screams. They can even make faces to communicate with each other and they purr to say hello.

Capuchins live in groups of about 10 to 40 adults, with several males, but most of them are related females who stay together, separate from the males, with the children. Babies are carried everywhere until they're 2 years old. Then, when they're toddlers, they're allowed to play nearby in the high branches of jungle trees, having fun running and leaping and chasing each other. Sometimes young Howler Monkeys play with them.

Nine different kinds of Capuchin Monkey live in Central and South America. The species in Costa Rica is called Carita Blanca – which means 'white face' in Spanish. All Capuchins have a tail as long as their body. They use it like a third hand to help them hang onto branches as they move through the forest and eat. Carita Blanca is a medium size monkey, about the size and weight of a cat. They are very strong and can live to be more than 50 years old.

They spend their life moving through and resting in the forest. They hunt for food from the forest floor up to the high treetops. Capuchins live in a variety of forests – tropical rainforests, dry forests and mangrove swamps – both high up in the hills and in the lowlands. They have a good chance of surviving deforestation, which is the removal of a forest's trees by humans, because they can live in so many different forest ecosystems.

Capuchin Monkeys need to drink a lot and have to be close to fresh water. They eat many things. On land they eat small animals, insects, spiders, and bird eggs as well as fruits, nuts, seeds and plant buds. When they live in mangrove swamps – which grow in shallow salt water – they also eat animals with shells, such as crabs. To get inside the shell they use stones to crack them open. Capuchins are very important for the health of all forests because they poop (and pee) from high in the trees, spreading important seeds to grow in new places. When you walk in a forest, be mindful of what's above you!

The beautiful Harpy Eagle, one of the world's largest and most dangerous birds of prey, along with boa constrictors and jaguars are a danger for Capuchins. Local people are also a danger as they also hunt them to eat; they call this 'bushmeat'. People also trap, sell and export Capuchins for scientific research and for the pet trade.

Most of an adult Capuchin's body is dark brown. Their head, face, neck, shoulders and upper chest are either white or light tan. The top of their head is black, like a cap. Each Capuchin, just like us, is an individual in personality and in appearance.

Warning: do not feed Capuchin Monkeys as some of our foods are poisonous to them.

CESARE
THE
CAPUCHIN MONKEY

PACIFIC
SCREECH OWL

PACIFIC SCREECH OWL

Megascops guatemalae

This is a young, little Pacific Screech Owl. All Screech owls are small and move quickly and there are two even smaller kinds of Screech Owl in Costa Rica. They all look similar but you can tell the species apart by small differences when they sing. Each bird also makes its song individual so that it's like no other owl's song.

Sounds and songs the owl makes are messages for other owls. A Pacific Screech Owl's song is 'who' sung 4 to 15 times quickly in a row. Who who who who who who who who who who who who who who who. These are called 'bouncing-ball notes'. They may be a warning saying 'stay away!' or they might just say, 'this is my home'. Sometimes they also add a deep warble at the end, or a trill, or go 'woof!' And they sometimes screech very loudly to warn off an attacker. Pacific Screech Owl families talk, back and forth, all night long. They're very social.

The female owl chooses her partner by judging the quality of the tree hole that he has chosen for a nest. She especially likes finding a nice meal for her inside it. They then sing very loudly, together. The mother owl lays 3-5 eggs in the dry season. The mother and father owl stay together, with their owlets, until early in the wet season.

The Pacific Screech Owl can only be found in the Americas, in a narrow strip of land along the Pacific Ocean coast, from Southern Mexico all the way down to Central Costa Rica. They live all their lives in a small area within this range and never migrate. Pacific Screech Owls can live to be 13 years old.

They spend their day roosting in a tree, on a bough, near the trunk where they are well camouflaged. At night, adults perch on a branch or a fence post out in the open away from the trunk, waiting to pounce on a large insect, a scorpion, or a small mouse to eat – or to fly after a moth. Their big ears, with stereoscopic hearing, and their big eyes, with night vision, help them to be nocturnal animals – to fly and hunt in the dark. They are fierce and accurate hunters. Sometimes they roost near houses to make use of the artificial light around them to better see their prey.

Trees are very important to the Pacific Screech Owl. They live in a wide variety of forests and in open spaces where there are scattered trees. The owls are often near roadsides, waterways, and on the edges of forests. They can live on forest land that has been very damaged by human use and, oddly, this will help ensure their survival.

Pacific Screech Owls use a clever flight and landing pattern to fool predators. They leave their nest by dropping down to fly near lower tree branches and then they make a U-turn to fly up and away. They return by flying in low and then they rise sharply up into their nesting area. If you watch a nest, you'll see them leave about the same time every day after sundown.

 When flying, they are often hit by cars or fly into buildings. Foxes and birds of prey, as well as house cats, hunt them. Their eggs are eaten by many other animals. Humans hunt them, poison them, and pollute their environment. They also get diseases and can starve. The number of Pacific Screech Owls hasn't ever been counted and so scientists don't know if their population is stable, and staying the same, or decreasing. Their safety depends on our protection of their forests and of the tree-corridors that connect these forests.

The Small Screech Owls' feathers have beautiful patterns. Their underparts are slightly paler than their upper-parts. Everywhere, all over their body except near their upper wing which has a white stripe, they have dark and light brownish, greyish, or sometimes reddish-brown streaks and wavy lines. Their eyelid rims are brownish-pink and their beak is greenish. Their eyes have a strikingly bright inner ring of orange and an outer ring of yellow.

ANGEL
THE
PACIFIC SCREECH OWL

WESTERN SPOTTED SKUNK

WESTERN SPOTTED SKUNK

Spilogale gracilis

Western Spotted Skunk mothers can give birth to six pups in a litter. The pups spend their first eight weeks with her in their underground den, a hole in the ground lined with leaves, while she keeps them warm and fed with her milk. After they're weaned off her milk, and can eat other things, she'll bring them fresh food. As omnivores, like us, they eat everything: fruit, insects, rodents and even scorpions. Their mother brings these home and teaches them how to hunt for food themselves. When they're ready to go out of the den they follow their mother in a line as they travel. They're nocturnal – out and about at night – and hide in their den during the day.

Outside, the pups play together – acting like adults – learning all the things they need to know to be safe after they leave home. They need to protect themselves from dogs and cats where people live and from panthers, bobcats and owls in the wild – and from humans everywhere. They have a special way to protect themselves by spraying predators with stinky musk from their rear ends.

They give a number of fair warnings to their attacker before they spray. They first raise their long tail and hiss. Then they will stamp their front paws (with long claws) and stand stiff and stare. They'll then strut around stomping the ground. Now they'll scratch the ground – and then charge! their attacker. If none of these tactics work to make the attacker leave it alone the skunk will do a hand-stand on its front paws, with its tail and back legs up in the air, and wave its rear end. If this final warning doesn't work they now put all their paws on the ground, turn around, and aim their rear at their attacker's eyes and squirt. This blinds their enemy long enough for them to run away. The smell of their musk on the attacker's hair or skin lasts for days and it's awful.

If your dog or cat comes home stinking of it you can wash them with 1 quart of 3% hydrogen peroxide mixed with 1/4 cup baking soda and 1 teaspoon of liquid soap. Skunks have an excellent sense of smell – they don't spray near their dens.

Other than mums and pups together, skunks live alone. In the winter, groups of females will snuggle together in a communal den. Skunks don't hibernate – they just slow down. Males usually spend the winter in their own den but sometimes the father joins his young family to rest and sleep, all together, until Spring.

The Western Spotted Skunk is about the size of a cat and it also moves like a cat. They're very slim and only weigh 1 to 3 pounds (0.4 to 1.3 liters). Their hair is long, soft, dark and glossy and each skunk has unique white spots – each Skunk is an individual, just as we are. They can't see more than 10 feet (3 m) away but they can hear very well.

They like to live in tall plants so that they can hide as they look for food. They also like to live near humans in developed areas, where there are buildings, and sometimes they even move into our attics.

Skunk populations are declining, most often due to human activities. They can live to be 10 years old but many of them die very young. They can't see cars coming on our roads. Pesticides, used to kill insects, kill them, too. And, as people don't like having den holes in their yard and fear being sprayed, people also kill them.

Skunks, though, can help us as they eat pests, like grasshoppers, in farmers' fields and they get rid of rodents – mice and rats – in our neighbourhoods.

Susi
THE
Western Striped Skunk

WHITE-NOSED COATI

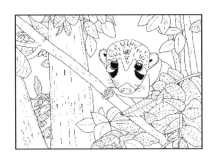

WHITE-NOSED COATI

Nasua nasua

The White-nosed Coati is a kind of raccoon that lives in Costa Rica. There it's called Pizote. They are adorable and especially clever and agile – they can figure things out, make the best of any situation and adapt, and they can even walk upside down while hanging from vines in the trees.

They are also very sociable and communicate in many ways. They talk with each other – squeaking, grunting, snorting, whining or screaming – all of the time. They warn other animals of a forest fire with a special, loud shriek. They brush and clean each other with their long front claws and their large sharp teeth while chirping in happiness. They hide their nose in their paws to back away from a fight and to prepare for a fight they show their teeth, lower their head and then jump at the threat.

During the daytime they hunt for food on the ground –where they spend most of their time – and up in trees, doing acrobatics. Pizotes can go up and down trees like squirrels because they're double jointed. They sleep in trees at night. If they're being hunted by humans, they find better places to hide and sleep.

When they live near humans they stay awake at night to go through the trash and look for food. Pizotes eat fruits and plants, insects and spiders, and any kind of meat. They also eat the endangered Olive Ridley Sea Turtle.

All adult male Pizote hunt and live alone except during the breeding season. The females and their kits (children) live together hunting, grooming, playing and relaxing. When a mother goes to hunt for food, the female group babysit her kits. Together, they also fiercely fight off predators.

When the kits are four months old they begin to play with all the other kits.

They chase each other up and down trees and play games while making lots of noise. Each Pizote is an individual and they can tell each other apart by their voice, how they look, and how they smell. They learn these things as children.

The males are twice as large as the females. They're about 43 inches long (109 cm) with a ringed tail that's longer than this. The tail can't hold on to branches or vines but it does help them keep their balance. Pizotes are about a foot tall (30 cm) and look very much like a large house cat. They weigh from two to seventeen pounds (1 to 8 kg) and they live to be seven to twelve years old.

They have a long flexible nose that they use in many ways. It helps them to push things around, get insects out of the ground, and to rub resin into their fur as an insect repellent.

Lately, although they prefer to live in forests, Pizotes have moved into cities looking for food. They're very intelligent and they don't mind being near us but it's against the law to feed wild animals in Costa Rica. If you do feed them, Pizotes may attack you when you don't feed them. They might also tip over your garbage cans or break into your home or campsite looking for food.

Pizote have been considered 'threatened' in some areas and of 'least concern' in other areas. But because scientific studies haven't been made of them in the wild, we really don't know how many Pizote there are now nor if they are now endangered.

Their forest homes have been cut down, their land and water has been polluted by our activities, and buildings have been built where they live and traffic. They are killed to protect farmers' crops and trapped to sell as pets. Some people even eat them. They are also hunted by large hunting birds, wild cats, weasels, foxes and boa snakes.

You can help the Pizote by not littering and by protecting wetlands, their water source.

Pepe

the

White-Nosed Coati

Costa Rican
Zebra Tarantula

COSTA RICAN ZEBRA TARANTULA

Aphonopelma seemanni

The Costa Rican Zebra Tarantula is also called the Striped Knee Tarantula. It's shy and nervous and it will quickly run away from you.

It looks beautiful, and it's not huge, but don't pick it up! It might bite you with its fangs. This is how it defends itself when it can't escape – and how it stuns its prey. Its poisonous fangs are under its head. The bite will be deep and hurt. But it will give you a warning first – either it will fling stinging hairs at your face with its back legs or it will stand up on its back legs and hiss. This spider may look scary but it isn't if you leave it alone.

The Zebra Tarantula lives on, and in, the forest floor. Each spider digs a deep burrow to live in, from 10 inches to 30 feet deep (25 cm to 9 m) and it then stays near its home. Usually there are many Zebra Tarantulas living in one area. Usually they only come out at night but when it's cloudy you can often find them outside of their burrows sunbathing to warm themselves. Sometimes they come out of their burrow at dusk. They especially like living on a grassy embankment, such as slopes of well-watered lawns, where the water won't go into their burrow and insects are easy to find and eat. But they can also be found in open forests and meadows and on pasture land, hillsides and cleared land.

A Tarantula has eight small eyes. They use smell, touch and vibration to find a mate. To help it feel its way while walking in the dark, it also uses its short front legs as if they were antennae.

They are wandering spiders and don't make a web. They wander about near their burrow, taking delicate steps on the forest floor, looking for prey to run and leap on. They eat all kinds of insects. While they hold onto their prey with their front legs, they poke their fangs deeply into their prey's body and ooze a poisonous, paralyzing venom into their meal. This venom turns their prey's insides to soup that they then suck up through their mouth straws. A good meal will last them a month.

Most male Zebra Tarantulas only live around five years but females can live up to 20 years. When fully grown, they're both about 4 to 5 inches long (10 to 12 cm) including their legs. This is about the same size as the palm of an adult human hand.

Its legs are black or dark brown. They have white to cream colored bands and long light-orange hairs.

The front part of the tarantula's body is called the prosoma. This is where its brain, jaws, small eyes and stomach are. It is the same color as the legs, with light orange hairs all around it. There is also a small bit of light-orange where each of its eight legs attach to the prosoma.

The back part of its body is called the abdomen. This is where its lungs, heart, and genitals are. It is also the same color as the rest of the body but with a lot more, and longer, reddish-orange hairs. The underbelly (hidden in this drawing) and the two little spinnerets at the end of the abdomen are bright orange.

Some of the Zebra Tarantula's body hairs can sense temperature, some can smell, and others can feel vibrations in the air.

So that they can grow, Zebra Tarantulas molt, or shed, their old 'skin'. This 'skin' is called an exoskeleton and it protects the spider. It's made out of layers of chitin, like our own nails are. If you find a Zebra Tarantula laying on its back, do not disturb it! This might kill it. It's remarkable that they can also regrow a missing leg while they are molting.

A spider spins fine lines of silk from its spinnerets. The silk is made inside its body. The tarantula spins 5 or 6 different kinds of silk for different uses such as to hide the entrance of its burrow and to softly line the burrow's walls. Some scientists think that the Zebra Tarantula also spins silk from its toes on its 8 hairy feet to help them cling to slippery surfaces as they climb – but other scientists think they just use the molecular charge on their feet hairs (like geckos do) to stick to walls. Zebra Tarantulas weigh very little otherwise they couldn't do this. They also have 2 little claws on each foot to hold onto things.

Because Zebra Spiders can live in so many places, are successful hunters of so many kinds of insects and smaller spiders, and aren't aggressive, they are less likely to become endangered as a species in the future. But it might already be in danger from habitat destruction everywhere it lives and from the collection of this beautiful, gentle spider from the wild for the illegal exotic pet trade.

Tara
the
Costa Rican
Zebra Tarantula

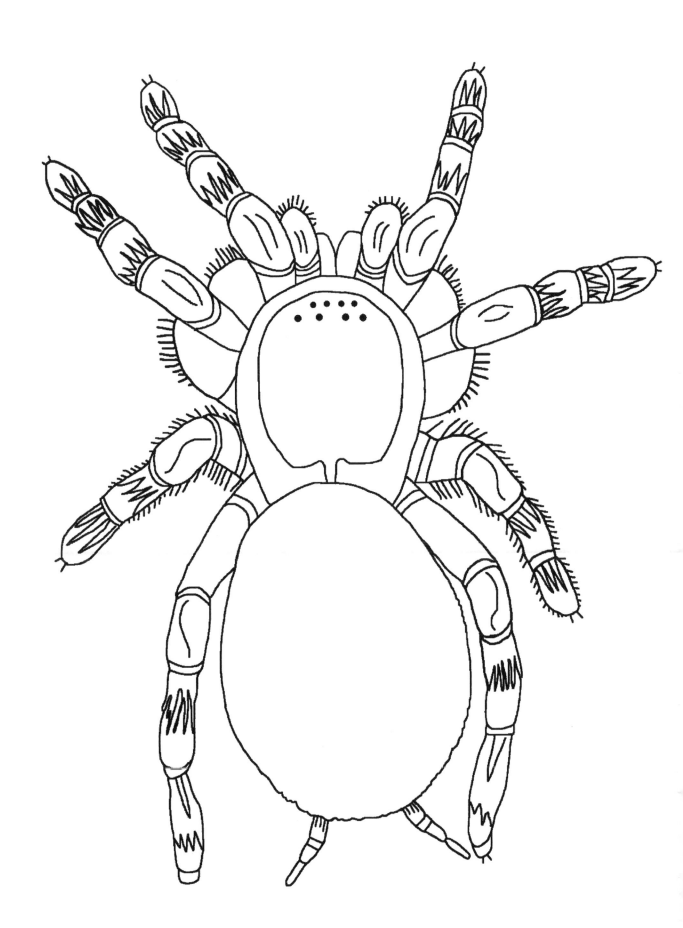

DAHLIA

DAHLIA

Dahlia pinnata

The Dahlia is native to the Middle American landbridge, from southern Mexico to northern South America. There are many different varieties of the genus Dahlia, with an incredible variety of flower sizes, colors, and arrangement of petals. There are 36 wild species and, because it's a natural hybrid whose genes can be mixed to create new forms, there are now at least 50,000 different kinds of dahlias created by plant breeders. New hybrids are introduced to the world every year. Dahlias are an excellent example of the amazing diversity of life in Central America.

Central America was a colony of Spain from the 16th to the 19th Century. Botanists travelled with Spanish Conquistadors looking for useful new kinds of plants. They took a Dahlia they'd found in Mexico back to Europe in the 17th century. This plant was the 20 feet tall Tree Dahlia which has a very simple flower. The ancient Aztec civilization ate Dahlia tubers, the part that grows underground, and may have also used them as medicine.

The Dahlia has been in cultivation in Europe since 1790, at first as a food crop. Europeans didn't find the tubers tasty but they did find them beautiful and so it was grown (from seed as well as from tubers) as a garden flower instead. It's now found in gardens all over the world.

Dahlias are easy to grow. They do well in a wide variety of soil types. They enjoy sunshine, a moist area with good drainage, and shelter from wind. They flower from late June to early December if the weather remains warm. They're perennials but die back after frost.

Dahlias don't have, or need, a smell. The bees and butterflies that pollinate Dahlias have excellent vision and visit dahlias because they're attracted to its bright colors.

Dahlia flowers grow on a bush. The flower can be 2 inches to more than 10 inches in diameter (5 to over 25cm). They are often pink, red, or orange but you can find them in every color – yellow, white, blue, and even green. Some have white tips on each petal. Some have a thin line of color outlining white petals or have white outlining coloured petals. Some have stripes of colour running from the outer tips of their petals to the flower's center. Some have a center that's a brighter color than the petals and others have a center that's the same color as the petals but darker.

My drawing shows a Dahlia pinnata; it looks like a pinwheel. It was one of three new kinds of Dahlia created from seeds sent to Spain's Royal Gardens of Madrid from Mexico's City's Botanical Garden in 1789. These were the first European hybrid Dahlias.

In 2015, a new collection of six Dahlia varieties was created by professional growers; they are now finally a food crop, vegetables! They're called DeliDahlias and both their flower and their tubers can be eaten. Each one is a beautiful carbohydrate. Fantastic looking white, orange, and red tubers can be eaten every way that you can prepare potatoes. Even better yet, each variety has its own flavor.

Types of DeliDahlias

Black Jack – red flower; tuber tastes like asparagus and kohlrabi

Buga Munchen – purple-pink flower; sweet tasting tuber, like parsley, and crisp

Fantastic – yellow-pink flower; tuber more neutral taste, slightly sour with smoky 'perfume'

Hoamatland – red and white; firm tuber tastes like black salsify

Kennedy – red flower; spicy flavored tuber tastes like fennel and celery

Sunset – orange-yellow flower; tuber tastes like kohlrabi

The Buga Munchen, Kennedy and Sunset varieties can be grown in containers.

After enjoying the DeliDahlias in your garden for their beauty, you can now also eat the young tubers at the end of their season just as the Aztecs did.

They are available from Lubera: **www.lubera.co.uk**

DAHLIA
PINNATA

COSTA RICA'S WILDLIFE

OVERVIEW

Costa Rica is part of an ancient wildlife 'land-bridge' that connects North and South America. We call this 'bridge' Central America. It rose from the Ocean about 3 million years ago but it may be much older; rocks over 100 million years old have been found in Costa Rica. Animals and plants use this bridge as their migratory pathway between the Northern and Southern Hemispheres. Many migrating animals stop and stay in Costa Rica for a while as seasonal visitors.

Amazingly, 5% of all the species on Earth can be found in Costa Rica. There are more species in Costa Rica than in any other place in the Americas.

There are at least 14,000 plant species and at least 500,000 animal species.

The numbers of species are approximations as we need more scientists to count them. Many more unknown species are seen but have not yet been studied. Some species have already gone extinct and new species are still being discovered!

There are about 50,000 dots below – imagine multiplying by ten to give you an idea of just how many different animal species can be found in Costa Rica!

Costa Rica's Plants

There are 10,000 species of <u>vascular plants</u> – this means that water moves inside them through roots, stems and leaves.

At least 2,000 of these are species of trees,

800 are species of ferns and

1,300 are species of flowering orchids.

There are also 4,000 species of <u>non-vascular plants</u> – these have no roots, stems or leaves.

They are mosses, liverworts and hornworts.

They are very small and need to live close to water.

Costa Rica's Land Animals

493,000 of the 500,000 animal species in Costa Rica are <u>invertebrates</u> – this means that they don't have a backbone.

1,800 of these invertebrate species are spiders, including the tarantula.

300,000 of these species are insects.

8,000 of the insect species are butterflies and moths.

13,000 are species of ants, bees and wasps.

20,000 are species of beetles.

About 7,000 species of Costa Rican animals have backbones; they are <u>vertebrates</u>.

There are 900 species of mammals.

40 of them are species of bats.

4 are species of monkeys, which are called New World Monkeys.

878 of these are species of birds.

16 of these are species of parrots.

About 200 of these are migrating species which visit every year.

221 of these are species of reptiles.

138 of these are species of snake.

22 are venomous species and

5 are powerful boa species.

There are 4 turtle species and many species of lizards, crocodiles and iguanas (the Green Iguana is 6 feet long (2 m) and lives in trees).

194 of these are species of amphibians.

165 of these are species of frogs.

COSTA RICA'S WATER ANIMALS

Costa Rica is between the Pacific Ocean and the Caribbean Sea with beaches and reefs on both sides. As the land bridge arose out of the ocean, the species on each side evolved differently into about 300 new species.

Coral reefs on both sides are rich with life that hasn't yet been recorded.

Future scientists exploring Costa Rica's marine life will make many exciting discoveries.

6,777 marine species have been recorded but the true number may be closer to 300,000.

There are 20 species of sea mammals – whales and dolphins – that migrate and spend some time in Costa Rican waters.

There are over 1,000 species of fresh and saltwater fish which is nearly 4% of all the fish species in the world.

There are 110 species of crabs, shrimps and lobsters.

LOCATION OF COSTA RICA AND SIBU

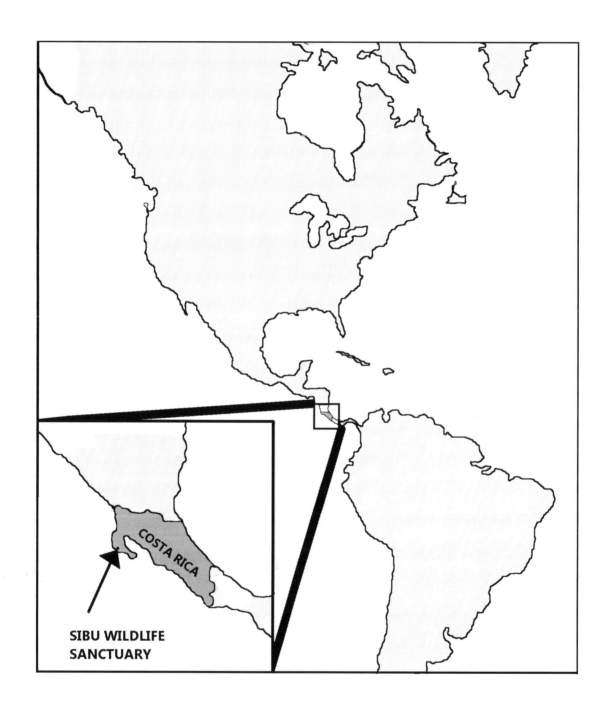

COSTA RICA

SIBU WILDLIFE
SANCTUARY

Costa Rica's Hotspots and Zones

Overview

Costa Rica is very biodiverse, complex, fascinating, beautiful and extremely important to all of us. Because of the many plants and animals and ecologies that are part of Costa Rica, scientists have included it in many of the ways they have ecologically divided the Earth.

HOTSPOTS

Plant and animal life is in danger everywhere on Earth but there are a few places where life is very rich, very diverse and unique, and very endangered. These are hotspots, places we need to pay attention to right now. Scientists aren't sure how many hotspots we have but we have at least 20 and perhaps 35. They have each lost 70-90% of their natural habitat due to our activities.

Costa Rica is part of the Mesoamerican Biodiversity Hotspot. It covers most of Central America, from central Mexico to the Panama Canal.

A portion of Costa Rica is also in the Western Caribbean Hotspot, which is in the Caribbean Sea and is made up of gorgeous coral reefs filled with many kinds of life.

ENDEMIC SPECIES AND ZONES

There are many endemic species in Costa Rica – these are species of plants and animals that live nowhere else on Earth. There are 3 endemic zones in Costa Rica. These are areas where, over a very long time, species couldn't leave because they were surrounded by barriers such as mountains, large bodies of water, or very dry places.

The Highlands Endemic Zone has mountain ranges and volcanoes and it's shared with Western Panama. The Southern Pacific Lowlands Endemic Zone is a moist, wet lowland rainforest – it's not on high ground like hills and mountains.

And the <u>Cocos Island Endemic Zone</u> is a part of the famous Galapagos Island Archipelago, 600 miles out in the Pacific.

Over time, because they couldn't leave to find new mates to reproduce with, some of the species in each area evolved into their very own new species. These are endemic. Endemic species are very special, very rare, and if they become endangered they are very likely to become extinct. A famous example of this was the endemic, beautiful, Golden Toad. It hasn't been seen in Costa Rica since 1989.

ECOZONES

An ecozone is a large area of the Earth where plant and animal species have evolved together. The Earth has 8 ecozones. Costa Rica is in the Neotropic Ecozone. It has both tropical and subtropical climates.

The Pacific side of this ecozone is very wet from storms, most of which are stopped by the mountain peaks where they then rain. The Atlantic side is both wet and dry. The areas at the top of the mountains are very wet, and are often cloudy and have fog.

ECOSYSTEMS

On land, Costa Rica has three kinds of jungle ecosystems: rainforest, cloud forest and tropical dry forest. There are also wetlands, savannahs (which are grasslands with a few trees), and mountains.

In Costa Rica there are 5 mountain ranges. They have 6 active volcanoes and 61 volcanoes that are inactive or extinct. The ranges are on two tectonic plates, large floating parts of the Earth's crust that cause earthquakes when they move. Each side of a mountain range has levels of different habitats with an exceptional variety and number of ecosystems. Most Costa Rican animals stay in Costa Rica and only migrate from one to another layer, up and down the mountain ranges, every year.

Costa Rica means 'rich coast' in Spanish and it has beautiful ecosystems near and in water, both on land and in the Ocean. Near the shore there are living coral reefs that are beautiful homes for a great variety of different kinds of marine species. There are also rare gentle, seagrass meadows off shore. On land there are beaches of small round stones called cobble – and beaches of sand, either white or black. And between the ocean and land, there are mangrove forests with long underwater roots where young fish can hide. These forests are where rivers meet the Ocean.

ECOREGIONS

There are 8 large ecoregions in this small country. These are geographical areas that have their own unique mixture of ecosystems, each with their own kinds of plants and animals, all working together.

THE TROPICAL DRY FOREST ECOREGION OF COSTA RICA

THE TROPICAL DRY FOREST

There are seven provinces in Costa Rica. SIBU Sanctuary is in the biologically important Guanacaste Province, the only province that has a <u>tropical dry forest ecoregion</u>. This kind of tropical forest is now even more rare in the world than the tropical rain forest is, which is probably what you think of as 'the jungle'.

There are many national parks with tropical dry rainforest. Two of the most important are the Guanacaste National Park, part of a natural migration pathway, and the Area de Conservacion Guanacaste , a UNESCO World Heritage Site.

Through modern planning and hard work – by local citizens, the Costa Rican government, and foreign conservation groups – Costa Rica's dry forest in Guanacaste now has a nearly intact, repaired, uninterrupted Pacific tropical dry forest. SIBU's tropical dry forest is one of the very few in Costa Rica that is not attached to the larger, uninterrupted tropical dry forest and so it is even more important to protect it.

About half of the year – from December through April – it doesn't rain in the tropical dry forest. Costa Rica is always warm but it is very hot from March to April. Plants and animals have survived this dry season through adaptations – those who survive pass on their genes.

Plants have found some interesting ways to retain water to use when there's no rain – many ground plants have thick leaves that store water to use when it's dry. Trees – the deciduous, broadleaf kind and not evergreen trees – drop their leaves to save on using water. Any rainwater during the dry season goes straight to their roots.

During the dry season, the undergrowth – the plant growth beneath the trees – grows to be thick because sunlight can now get through the bare tree tops, through the forest canopy, to the forest floor. Flowers bloom and fruits grow in the dry season. This is a good time to see animals in the trees but a difficult time to see animals in the thick under-brush, beneath the trees. When the leaves return in the wet season, especially in September and October, the tree inhabitants are now more difficult to find and finding animals on the land is easier.

Many animals go into a summer-time hibernation, called estivation. They wake up when the rain returns. Monkeys, however, move to year-round damp areas where the trees still have leaves to eat. Howler Monkeys move to stream beds; they cram together and share the leaves and a bit of fruit with each other without fighting. When the rains return, leaves grow again on trees in drier areas and the Howlers move back to them.

When the forest blooms at the end of the rainy season, fantastic looking flowers compete to attract the most pollinators to help them make seeds to create new plants. Both insects and animals act as pollinators – they move male pollen around to fertilize female flowers. During this time the jungle is full of color! This interaction to keep the forest growing has to be perfectly timed, so that both hungry insects and blooming plants happen at the same time.

There are 3,140 species of butterflies and moths – and 400 species of plants to be pollinated here.

Many insects have relationships with specific plant species and they need each other to continue to exist. The seeds that come from pollination, such as nuts, are also a major food source for many animals. This process is very important for the health of the dry forest ecosystem.

If any part of it is removed, the entire system becomes endangered.

DANGERS TO THE TROPICAL DRY FOREST ECOREGION

The dry forest ecosystem has been lived in and used by humans for at least 11,000 years. We've done a lot of damage to it in that time and although many concerned people, groups, and the Costa Rican government have worked hard to restore ecosystems there are still many threats which might push ecosystems, and species, to extinction.

Climate change, pollution, forest clearing by cutting and burning, and people building on clearings are big ecological issues everywhere in the world.

In 2016, the species in this coloring book weren't currently thought to be very endangered but this is most likely to change when their populations are counted again by the IUCN (which is trying to raise funding to do this). There are already extra dangers for the animals at SIBU.

They have to deal with unsheathed electrical wires and power generators. Arboreal (tree) animals think they are vines to travel on, and when they touch them they get electrocuted and badly burned. And when parts of their environment, such as trees and vines, have been removed they then have to cross roads to travel and are then often killed by traffic and dogs.

Pollution of all kinds, from everything we do, is a danger everywhere in the world. Plastic waste is a pollution we can see. It strangles animals by filling their hungry stomachs with many bits of small bits of plastic waste that they can't digest and then die from. Many local people eat these animals, who have eaten these poisonous tiny bits.

By living closer to us, so that they can use our night lighting and enjoy our yummy garbage, small wild animals are put in danger of being caught by bigger animals. Even humans catch them to sell as pets or to sell to zoos or to eat them.

ORGANIZATIONS
SAVING WILDLIFE
IN COSTA RICA

This book is based on the SIBU Wildlife Sanctuary. There are a few other very busy Costa Rican wildlife rescue and sanctuary organizations that are non-profit, privately owned, and rely on donations. Two of them are the Fundacion Santuario Silvestre de Osa and The Tree Of Life Wildlife Rescue Center and Botanical Gardens. I think you might be delighted with all three of these amazing rescue groups and so their information is below. It will be wonderful if you help them to continue their valuable work protecting the wildlife of Costa Rica, a beautiful part of the vitally important Mesoamerican Biodiversity HotSpot.

SIBU Wildlife Sanctuary

SIBU Wildlife Sanctuary is a privately owned non-profit wildlife sanctuary. It's on the edge of the larger, privately owned Nosara Biological Reserve in Costa Rica. They work together as loving, caring, rescue centers for animals who have been hurt just because they live near humans. All of the Howler monkeys, the Western Spotted Skunk, the White Faced Capuchin, the White-nosed Coati, and the Little Screech Owl in this book are rescued animals at SIBU. They were found hurt and then brought to SIBU to be given around-the-clock medical care and comforting. Vicki and Steve have given them a temporary home in the SIBU sanctuary, along with many other recovering animals – while still allowing them to be wild. Their rehabilitation will last until they're ready to be released back into the wild reserve. If they can't be released, they then have a life-long home at SIBU.

SIBU welcomes your heart-felt care for their patients and it hopes you will visit them, help by volunteering, and give your support. You can help them by buying a transformer insulation kit, by helping them build a new nursery and by adopting one of the adorable monkeys at SIBU. Every bit of your help goes towards helping wounded wildlife in a very important, beautiful tropical dry forest – one of our world's most endangered hotspot treasures. Thank you.

From SIBU Wildlife Sanctuary's website:

> SIBU Wildlife Sanctuary's mission is to rescue injured, orphaned and displaced wild animals and provide them immediate medical care, rehabilitation, and eventual release into the wild. When the animals are determined to be strong, healthy and old enough to be re-integrated into the jungle they begin a step-down release program. Animals unlikely to survive in the wild receive a permanent enriching habitat for their life-term care.

We are also educators and advocates who work cooperatively with other organizations to encourage respect for animals' lives and preservation of their habitat. We rehabilitate animals with assistance from veterinary and wildlife specialists and work closely with Costa Rica's electric company (ICE) to prevent electrocutions.

Visit SIBU: *http://sibusanctuary.org/visit-sibu/*

Reservations required, in advance

During your visit you will:

Walk to the North Ridge of the Sanctuary for beautiful views while learning about the local ecology, geology, flora and fauna

Learn the history of SIBU Sanctuary

Relax in the Educational Pavilion as Vicki explains the issues that threaten Costa Rica's wildlife and our efforts to mitigate their impact

Observe first-hand the extensive amount of work required to operate a wildlife rescue, rehabilitation and release center

Visit the monkey habitats to observe their behavior, social interactions, and anatomy

To visit you must have been in Costa Rica for 3 or more days and be in good health.

Monkeys are so closely related to humans that they catch many of the same sicknesses that we do, so to help reduce the risk of transmitting germs to our residents we ask that you please respect this very important requirement. For this same reason, any form of contact with the animals is prohibited.

Volunteer Program: *http://sibusanctuary.org/volunteer-at-sibu/*

To Help SIBU

http://sibusanctuary.org/donate

Help build a New Sanctuary and Educational Center:
http://sibusanctuary.org/donate/donations/nursery-quarantine-facility-project/

Help the 'Stop the SHOCKS!' project:
http://sibusanctuary.org/donate/donations/stop-the-shocks-project/

Help by adopting a Monkey: *http://sibusanctuary.org/adopt-a-monkey/*

Contact

Facebook: *https://www.facebook.com/SIBUWildlifeSanctuary*

SIBU Wildlife Sanctuary
Nosara, Guanacaste, Costa Rica

E-mail *SIBUcr@gmail.com Jungalow@gmail.com*

Telephone numbers (Costa Rica Only) 6 a.m. – 6 p.m. CST

506-8413-8889 506-8866-4652

The Tree Of Life Wildlife Rescue Center And Botanical Gardens

From their website:

The TREE OF LIFE, a many branched tree, illustrates the idea that all life is interconnected.

El ARBOL DE VIDA, un arbol de muchas ramas, significa que toda vida esta interconnectada.

We provide a safe haven to animals that need refuge because of loss of habitat, accidents and as victims of pet trade or hunting. Many of these animals can be nursed back to a healthy condition and can be released back into their natural habitat. Some animals have to stay with us and for these we try to provide the most natural habitat possible.

The gardens are approximately 10 acres of many types of plant groups. There are palms, heleconias, bromeliads, calatheas, aroids etc. There are a lot of different palm species and a special Talamanca area with indigenous plants. There are also spices like vanilla, black pepper and cinnamon. In addition we have papaya, banana, cacao and pineapple growing.

We have a breeding program for turtles and iguanas and we do reintroduce them to their natural habitat.

We promote conservation by activities of environmental education for the local schools. THINK GLOBALLY, START LOCALLY. There is a lot to see and it all makes for a fun and educational time. COME AND SEE US!

Gallery of Animals: http://www.treeoflifecostarica.com/animals.php

Support/ Donations

Tree of Life Wildlife Rescue Center & Botanical Gardens is an organization that does not receive any governmental funding. This means that donations and admission sales help the rescue center stay a home to all of its animals. Please support us in caring for the animals and maintaining the park facilities. THANKS.

If you would like to know more about the plant and animal life of Costa Rica, call to make a reservation for a personal tour.

Contact

Location: *Playa Grande, Cahuita, Costa Rica (follow the signs)*

Tel: *+506 83170325 or +506 27550014*

E-mail: *treeoflifecostarica@hotmail.com*

Facebook: facebook.com/TreeOfLifeWildlifeRescueCenterBotanicalGardens

Welcome and hope to see you soon!

Fundacion Santuario Silvestre De Osa

From their website:

FUNDACION SANTUARIO SILVESTRE DE OSA, also known as OSA WILDLIFE SANCTUARY (OWS), is a wildlife sanctuary and rescue center located north of Puerto Jimenez, across the Golfo Dulce. They are contiguous to Piedras Blanca NP and are accessible only by boat. We

- provide the best care possible for injured, orphaned and displaced wildlife, with the ultimate goal of rehabilitation and release when appropriate

- provide a public education program to promote conservation and the protection and enhancement of local habitat

- maximize the economic benefits for the local community through helping local eco-tourism operators with programs and services and by hiring local people

- offer volunteer internships

- promote comprehensive field surveys, natural history studies, and long-term observation of released animals

- offer free spayed and neuter clinics in the pueblos around Piedras Blancas NP

- support governmental agencies in their effort to enforce existing wildlife laws and regulations.

- and promote the care and preservation of habitats and ecosystems.

So many animals come to us with special needs. Your dollars help us care for many animals that would otherwise not survive. Your support allows us to feed, rehabilitate and sometimes release healthy animals back into the wild.

We spend many hours ensuring that all our animals have proper nutrition and the best life possible, but this is not possible without your much-needed support.

Please send your tax-deductible donations to:

OSA WILDLIFE SANCTUARY FOUNDATION INC.,
PO Box 171,
Greenwood, IN 46143
USA.

Phone:
001.506.8861.1309
011.506.8348.0499
E-mail: osa.carol@gmail.com

You can make your tax deductible donation through PayPal on the Foundation website http://www.osatest.org/

My Fat Fox

My Fat Fox is a small independent publisher of books and digital media. We are in love with our world and hope to encourage others to fall in love with it too.

More from My Fat Fox

Endangered Lizards Colouring Book
Endangered Frogs Colouring Book
Illustrated by Jay Manchand

Colour to Save the Ocean – Book One and Book Two
Illustrated by Kasia Niemczynska

Color and Save the Ocean – Book One
Party Animals Coloring Book – Moluccan Cockatoos – Mollywood
Illustrated by Karin Hoppe Holloway

Color Funny Doodles – Book One – Humorous
Color Funny Doodles – Book Two – Beautiful
Illustrated by Hartmut Jager

Frog Art Coloring Book – Volume One
Illustrated by Children Around the World for Frogs Are Green!

Where Do the Swallows Go?
Endangered Animals Colouring Book – UK Amphibians and Reptiles
Illustrated by Cassie Herschel-Shorland

Alan the Hedgehog (as Super Alan) in Color Me Alan!
Illustrated by Jon Hitchman

Visit **www.myfatfox.co.uk** for competitions, news and information on our latest publications. All our Earth Art Colouring Books will soon also be available as Earth Art Apps.

Made in the USA
San Bernardino, CA
05 October 2016